ARTISTIC
LEATHER WORK

A HANDBOOK ON THE ART OF DECORATING LEATHER

BY

E. ELLIN CARTER

British Library Cataloguing-in-Publication Data
A catalogue record for this book is available from the
British Library

Contents

Leather Crafting

Leather is a durable and flexible material created by the tanning of animal rawhide and skin, often cattle hide. It can be produced through manufacturing processes ranging from cottage industry to heavy industry, and has formed a central part of the dress and useful accessories of many cultures around the world. Leather has played an important role in the development of civilisation from prehistoric times to the present, and people have used the skins of animals to satisfy fundamental (as well as not so essential!) needs such as clothing, shelter, carpets and even decorative attire. As a result of this importance, decorating leather has become a large past time. Leather crafting or simply leathercraft is the practice of making leather into craft objects or works of art, using shaping techniques, colouring techniques or both. Today, it is a global past time.

Some of the main techniques of leather crafting include:

Dyeing - which usually involves the use of spirit- or alcohol-based dyes where alcohol quickly gets absorbed into moistened leather, carrying the pigment deep into the surface. 'Hi-liters' and 'Antiquing' stains can be used to add more definition to patterns. These have pigments that will break away from the higher points of a tooled piece and so pooling in the background areas give nice contrasts. This leaves parts unstained and also provides a type of contrast.

Painting - This differs from leather dyeing, in that paint remains only on the surface whilst dyes are absorbed into the leather. Due to this difference, leather painting techniques are generally not used on items that can or must bend, nor on items that receive friction, such as belts and wallets - as under these conditions, the paint is likely to crack and flake off. However, latex paints can be used to paint flexible leather items. In the main though, a flat piece of leather, backed with a stiff board is ideal and common, though three-dimensional forms are possible so long as the painted surface remains secured. Unlike photographs, leather paintings are displayed without a glass cover, to prevent mould.

Stamping - Leather stamping involves the use of shaped implements (stamps) to create an imprint onto a leather surface, often by striking the stamps with a mallet. Commercial stamps are available in various designs, typically geometric or representative of animals. Most stamping is performed on vegetable tanned leather that has been dampened with water, as the water makes the leather softer and able to be compressed with the design. After the leather has been stamped, the design stays on the leather as it dries out, but it can fade if the leather becomes wet and is flexed. To make the impressions last longer, the leather is conditioned with oils and fats to make it waterproof and prevent the fibres from deforming.

Molding and shaping - Leather shaping or molding consists of soaking a piece of leather in hot or room temperature water to greatly increase pliability and then shaping it by hand or with the use of objects or even molds as forms. As the leather dries it stiffens and holds its shape. Carving and stamping may be done prior to molding. Dying however, must take place after molding, as the water soak will remove much of the colour. This mode of leather crafting has become incredibly popular among hobbyists whose crafts are related to fantasy, goth / steampunk culture and cosplay.

PLATE I

CHAIR. UPHOLSTERED IN CUT, MODELLED, AND STAINED COWHIDE.

Awarded Gold Medal at Imperial International Exhibition, London, 1909

(Registered Design.)

PREFACE

I HAVE been persuaded, rather unwillingly, to compile this little handbook for the use of Art-Leather workers; but it must be clearly understood that, in doing so, I make no claim to literary ability even of a modest kind, and that my sole aim is practically to assist those who desire to acquire the art I love so well.

Years ago, as a novice, I searched frequently for a really useful book on the subject, but I searched in vain. Of the few volumes published, some were too costly, others were remarkable rather for verbosity than for practical utility. When, therefore, a pupil sought my advice in obtaining the means of becoming more perfect in the Art, I had to admit that I knew of no suitable work, and all I could do was to give a few written notes based on personal experience and research. It is from these notes that the following pages are compiled.

Whilst many branches of Leather Decoration are touched upon, it will be noted that the more detailed instructions are given in reference to "incised work." This is simply because, not only does such work need greater care to obtain success, but also because it is often the foundation of more elaborate work, and, in combination with staining, is capable of yielding remarkably artistic effects, even where little or no relief-work is attempted.

With these few words I commend this little book to the forbearance and goodwill of the reader.

———————

PREFACE TO SECOND EDITION

I HAVE been given considerable encouragement in the publishing of a second edition of this small guide by the fact that numbers of readers are continually writing to thank me for the benefit they have received from its pages. Especially does this apply to those who, living abroad, have not the opportunity of receiving personal tuition. I am both grateful for the exceedingly kind and generous way in which the first edition has been received, and hopeful that the second may prove equally helpful to others in need of similar guidance.

E. ELLIN CARTER.

ARTISTIC
LEATHER WORK

CHAPTER I

INTRODUCTORY NOTES

THERE is an indescribable but very definite charm in the smooth, soft-tinted surface of a well-dressed skin of leather, particularly of calf-skin. It is so full of possibilities, and the modelling of it to express one's ideas undoubtedly becomes more and more fascinating with practice. One can imagine such a skin in the deft hands of an enthusiast, first covered with a mysterious combination of angles, circles, and geometric figures, ultimately resulting in one of those beautiful designs one finds in the British Museum or the Paris Salon, etc. Let such beauty of design be the guiding principle even on the simplest work! The aim of every student in Leather Work (as indeed in all crafts) should be to avoid producing anything which lacks good workmanship, whilst the finished article should disclose the individuality of the worker—a result imparted only by the personal touch and observation of the true craftsman. Herein lies the difference between hand and machine work. When mind and hand act together, the best results are likely to be attained, for the worker then gives his individual attention throughout alike to the conception and execution of the design. In machine products, on the other hand, the personal touch is practically obliterated in the various processes employed, so that, however perfectly the work is executed, it never loses evidence of its mechanical production or acquires the charm of handwork. Given a work-bench in some corner that is one's very own, plus enthusiasm, patience, proper tools, a nice piece of leather, and a high ideal—and what may not be accomplished? It is easy to describe processes, however important, to explain that this tool is used to produce this effect, or that colour to produce that, but these count for little compared with the underlying creative principles at the root of all good work. However fair one's technique, it should never be forgotten that the process is *the means*, not the end; it is *the thought, the conception*, at the back of the expression, which stamps the work as either vital or lifeless.

PLATE II

A.—CARVED WORK.

B.—EMBOSSED WORK.

But let us proceed. There are different methods of decorating leather, and the student should decide before commencing work which style of treatment he will adopt. They include the following:—

I. *Cut or Incised Work.*—In this, the outlines of the design are cut with a sharp, pointed knife, to about one-third of the thickness of the leather, the incision being then opened out, and the details modelled with a proper tool. (*See* Plate III, A.)

II. *Embossed Work.*—The incised line may be used, or the outline only, firmly defined with the edge of the modeller. The design is raised on the surface of the leather entirely by pressure from the back, and is then modelled with brass or steel modelling tools, as in wax or clay, and finally padded with some suitable material. (*See* Plate II, B.)

III. *Modelled Work.*—This is really the most artistic treatment, and is worked with tools called modellers, just as one works in wax or clay, and can be carried to great perfection. (*See* Plate III, B.) A specimen of combined incised and modelled work is shown in Plate III, C.

IV. *Carved Work.*—In this method the design is incised, but the cut is made much deeper than in simple incised work, so that the body of the design stands out sufficiently to allow of its being ornamented by other lines less deeply worked. Great expertness is required and it should only be attempted by the experienced worker. (*See* Plate II, A.)

V. *Hammered or Punched Work.*—Leather decorated by means of punches is called hammered work. It is supplemental to other methods, and is used with advantage in the backgrounds of other forms of decoration. (*See* Plates V and VI.)

VI. *Mosaic Work.*—This is done by the superposition of a design cut out in very thin leather, on a groundwork of another colour.

There are other methods of leather decoration, but the beginner should confine his attention to the above. Such difficult processes as engraved or open-work, together with finishing in gold or silver, may well be omitted from the present volume.

CHAPTER II

TOOLS AND MATERIALS

Tools.—The first step to be taken by the student is to obtain a small supply of leather and the necessary tools, which are neither numerous nor expensive.

A slab of marble or lithographic stone about one inch thick, of convenient size for working on, say 15″ by 10″ or 12″ by 12″, must be purchased, as well as a cutting or incising knife, a tracing tool, one or two modelling tools, an opener, a brass foot-rule, a transparent 45° set square, and a good hard lead pencil. Then for colouring work, a small soft sponge, two or three fine rags, a supply of colouring materials (described further on), and three or four camel's hair brushes, will enable the beginner to produce some very good work.

It may be well also to include a small hammer, such as is used by metal workers, and three or four punches (to begin with), for hammered or punched backgrounds. Wheels are sometimes used for lines, but the novice may easily do what is required with the edge of the modelling tool and may use a beveller for broader lines. A screw-crease is a useful tool for lines quite close to the edge of the work. The use of the different tools will be explained later on. All that are necessary for a beginner are as follows :—

Tracer	Set square
Modeller	Hammer
Knife (or inciser)	Sponge
Opener	Saucers
Punches	Brushes
Ruler	Stains

Leather.—Great care is necessary in the choice of leather for decorative work.

The texture must be fine and supple, the surface free from blemishes and evenly tanned, and the skin of sufficient thickness to allow for deep modelling. For embossing, a thin skin is needed. If surface colouring is employed, it is highly important to select a leather in the tanning process of which nothing of a fatty nature has been used. It is extremely annoying, when one has spent hours, perhaps days, or even weeks in working a design to find that the leather will not receive colours properly, and that a dirty, mottled appearance is the only result obtainable. Firms who make a specialty of leather for decorative work are fully aware of this danger, and, as a rule, stock only such skins as have been properly prepared; it is therefore best to purchase from them, even though more expensive, rather than from an ordinary leather dealer whose skins may be very good but quite unsuitable.

The best skins for general artistic decorative work are calf or cowhide. Calf varies both in thickness and colour, but the advantage of great malleability more than counterbalances this objection. In selecting a skin, it should be borne in mind that, whilst high relief can be obtained best by using thick leather well damped, a thin skin, on the other hand, ensures a more delicate outline.

Cowhide is sold with either a polished or a dull surface; the latter is specially suited for decorative work, as the surface is more malleable and better adapted for modelling. For very large designs, cowhide should always be used in preference to calf.

Other skins used in the decoration of leather are as follows:—

Sheepskin (or Basil).—This is cheaper than any other leather, and may be used by the beginner for experimental work; but it does not lend itself very well to incising or carving, nor does it give very good colour results, so that it is unsuitable for fine work.

Morocco and Russia.—Both these are much used for fine book-work, as they are exceedingly durable and tough; and Russia is well adapted for wax modelling. Undressed morocco can also be obtained for modelling, and is most effective.

Vellum.—This is useful principally for brush or pen work. This class of decoration is beautiful enough, but does not come within the sphere with which we propose to deal.

Prices of Leather for Working.—Prices are greatly advanced since the war and are constantly varying. It is therefore useless to quote definite figures. Students sending stamped addressed envelope to the writer can always obtain current prices.

Dyes and Patines.—Practical knowledge is the only reliable guide in the selection of colouring fluids suitable for our purpose, for, whatever their base may be, all vary greatly in use. There are some aniline dyes which are more durable than vegetable dyes, whilst others, beautiful enough in themselves, fully maintain the reputation aniline has for instability.

The colours used for dyeing leather cannot be expected to remain unaffected by direct sunlight, but with ordinary care, the dyes we recommend should not fade materially for some considerable time.

We will not mystify the reader with technical descriptions of the various agents which have from time to time been used, especially as we strongly recommend the beginner to be satisfied—at first, at any rate—with a few bottles of ready-prepared fluids, and to use them in the manner hereinafter explained.

Four-ounce bottles of the leading colours, say dark blue, light blue, bright green, olive green, nut brown, dark brown, yellow, bright red, and Indian red, will suffice for most ordinary designs. It may, however, be useful and convenient to offer the following brief remarks.

Black is best produced by a wash of sulphate of iron over another of potash.

White cannot be produced on leather unless painted on as an enamel.

Brown is principally obtained from washes of potash; catechol and xanthin are also used.

Grey results from a solution of permanganate of potash, but this is rather uncertain in its action.

Blues.—The best are obtainable from indigo or alizarin, the colouring principle of madder.

Greens.—All ready-made greens are fugitive; the best results are obtained by applying alternate washes of blue and yellow. Olive green is produced by successive applications of solutions of sulphate of iron and picric yellow.

Reds.—The best are made from alizarin, but logwood, cochineal and cantharamine are sometimes used.

Yellows.—The base of most yellows is picric acid, a very powerful agent; the chromates of baryta and zinc are often used, especially in mixing greens.

Orange is best obtained by using red over yellow, or orange dyes prepared with alizarin may be used.

Pink is obtained from carthamine, which is the colouring matter of *carthamus tinctorius.*

Ordinary water-colours based on albumen or glycerine can be used in leather work, but spirit-colours possess a transparency which allows of their use over a ground previously covered with a different shade. French leather workers largely employ *Patines*, which produce a groundwork of great brilliancy if well rubbed before they are quite dry. (The word "patine" means a veneer or wash of colour applied to intensify the tone or to give artificial effects, such as those of antiquity or rust.)

PLATE III

A.—INCISED WORK.

B.—MODELLED WORK.

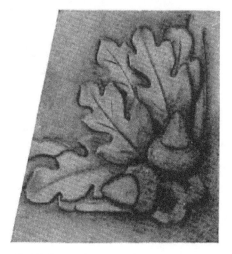

C.—INCISED AND MODELLED WORK.

Colours obtained from potash and sulphate of iron are much used for groundwork. The former produces a warm brownish red, the latter a variety of tints from a pale to a dark slate grey.

CHAPTER III

DIFFERENT METHODS OF DECORATING LEATHER

Preparing and Tracing the Design on to the Leather.—
Having equipped himself with suitable tools and materials, the
student will be anxious to commence operations. Whichever
method is selected, the first step is to obtain a suitable design,
and to transfer this to the surface of the leather. The process
is identical in all methods, so we shall describe it here, once
for all.

In selecting a design, a bold, effective outline without too
many small elaborate details should be chosen, such as those
shown on the following pages.

Whether or not the reader has studied design, he or she can—
by a judicious combination of geometric forms, curves, circles,
squares, triangles—make some kind of pattern on a sheet of
paper. If such a drawing is made in charcoal, the result is freer
than with pencil, and it would be better to make a sketch first
on a somewhat larger scale than is to be used, dispensing as
far as possible with ruling, tracing, or measuring. The natural
irregularities will only add strength.

*FIG. I.—SIMPLE DESIGN FOR A LAMP-MAT OR
SHAVING-CASE.*

Over the finished design place a sheet of tough tracing paper, or better still, architect's tracing linen, and, with drawing-pins, fix the two on to a drawing-board or smooth surface. With a hard lead pencil or drawing-pen make a careful tracing of the finished drawing. This done, place the linen tracing on to the leather, the two being held firmly together with clips close to the edge so that they cannot become displaced. A simple way is to turn a narrow piece of the top edge of the tracing material over one edge of the leather, and place clips at the four corners so that they do not interfere with the progress of the work; this will permit the traced design to be partly lifted when required for examination of the work.

FIG. 2. TRACING TOOL.

Now take the tracing tool, and go carefully over every line, pressing gently and evenly so as to produce a slight indentation of the surface of the leather, clearly visible to the eye. This is more successfully accomplished if the leather is from time to time slightly moistened with water; but when doing this in the first instance, care should be taken to moisten *the entire surface*, as otherwise an ugly aureole may be produced which is not easy to remove; after the first moistening this is not likely to occur, and portions of the surface may be damped without injury.

FIG. 3.—DESIGN FOR A PHOTO-FRAME OR BOOK-COVER.

An oval may be cut out in centre for photo, or a monogram may be worked in for a book-cover. The berries may be modelled, or stamped with punch.

During the progress of the work the tracing should be occasionally raised, to see that the design is well defined on the leather: should the lines be faint, it is proof either that the pressure on the pointer is insufficient, or that the surface is too dry and requires moistening again.

Having completed the transfer of the design to the leather, the tracing is to be removed, and the leather placed on the slab of marble or lithographic stone in order to commence the work of decoration which we now proceed to describe.

Incised Work.—Incising may be made very attractive without modelling, by adding colour or punching, or both. We shall here only describe the method of incising, leaving the colouring and punching to later Chapters. The first step is to cut the principal outlines in such a manner that the design may, after modelling, appear as if raised on the surface of the leather.

FIG. 4.—CUTTING (OR INCISING) KNIFE.

There are two kinds of knife used in doing this, both of which are illustrated in Figs. 4 and 5. It is a mere matter of individual choice which is selected, but with either of them great care must be taken to ensure that the incision is *absolutely vertical*. With knife shown in Fig. 4 the cut is made by drawing the knife *downwards*, towards the operator, much in the same way that one uses a pencil; the knife illustrated in Fig. 5 must be kept perfectly upright and gently pressed *upwards* and onwards with the second finger of the left hand, as shown in Fig. 6. The result in both cases should be the same, viz., a clean sharp incision, absolutely vertical, and plainly visible to the eye, as, unless it is so, the subsequent moulding cannot be successfully accomplished. The depth of the incision should vary according to the effect to be produced by subsequent operations, but should never exceed one-third of the thickness of the skin.

FIG. 5.–CUTTING (OR INCISING) KNIFE.

A little experience will enable the operator to form a correct judgment in regard to this.

FIG. 6.—POSITION OF HANDS FOR FORWARD CUT-TING.

In making curved lines, the left hand should be used to turn the leather gently round, so that it may always be in the most favourable position for the operation of the knife; the knife itself should not be turned. Two converging lines should not be cut quite up to the point of intersection, even in thick leather. The cut should just stop short of that point, and the line be subsequently continued with the modelling tool; otherwise, the strip of leather within the angle of the converging lines is apt to turn up and produce an unsightly effect.

Should it be desired to get the effect of the superposition of an object—say a leaf or flower—lying upon, but not part of, the background, the knife may be slightly slanted outwards, so that the edge of the leather may be raised a little and turned up as shown in Fig. 10.

Having finished the incising, the tool next to be used is called an Opener, and is shaped as shown below:—

FIG. 7.—OPENING TOOL.

Such tools can be had in various sizes and shapes to produce lines of different widths, but, for the beginner, one or at most a couple are sufficient, and we should prefer that illustrated. This somewhat resembles a modeller broadened in the centre and with a blunt point, or a small blade with the point ground away and angles rounded. *Some workers prefer to use only the edge of a fine modeller.* Before using the opener, the leather must be rendered malleable by being well moistened with sponge and water. A few seconds should be allowed for the water to sink into the surface, and the edge of the opener should then be inserted in an incision, and pressed gently forward with a slight gliding motion, the broad or round part of the tool being kept outwards so as to press the outer edge of the incision downwards; when opened the incision should have the appearance shown in Fig. 8.

31

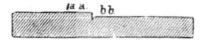

FIG. 8.

AN INCISION PROPERLY OPENED.

FIG. 9.

BADLY MADE SLANTING CUT.

The tool should be worked upwards and downwards in the opened cut, to ensure that the edges are well and evenly parted. We have already emphasised the importance of a *perfectly vertical cut*; let us draw the reader's attention to the accompanying four little drawings. Fig. 8 shows a properly made cut, with the background depressed; it will be seen that the part *a a* stands well above *b b*, thus producing the effect of relief. Fig. 9 is a badly made or slanting cut, which it is almost impossible to open properly, for on attempting this the point *c c* will curl up, and the result will be far from pleasing.

Such an incision, however, in a modified form, is shown in Fig. 10, which is correct enough when it is desired to produce the effect of superposition already referred to.

Incisions too deeply cut, as in Fig. 11, are likely, when the work is finished, to show a white line between the modelled portion and the background, consequent on the exposure of the inner substance of the leather. A similar line is also likely to appear if the modelling is not done tolerably soon after the incising and opening, or if the incisions are too widely opened. When such a defect unfortunately shows itself, the only way is to stain the line to match the surface of the leather, but the result is seldom quite satisfactory.

FIG. 10.
SLANTING CUT TO PRODUCE EFFECT OF SUPERPO-
SITION.

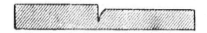

FIG. 11. CUT TOO DEEPLY.

FIG. 12.—SIMPLE DESIGN FOR LADIES'
CARD-CASE OR POCKET-BOOK.

Embossed Work.—This is one of the simplest forms of decoration, and does not necessarily require that the student should have previous artistic experience. It is more or less mechanical, and an artistic temperament will instinctively avoid it on this account for the more subtle and fascinating treatment displayed in surface modelling. At the same time, those with little time at their disposal may obtain very good effects from embossing. The work may be commenced either with or without the incised line to the design, as already explained. If it is used, the opening must be made after the embossing. If without, the design must be carefully and clearly defined with the edge of the modelling tool. It is not advisable to cut (or incise) when thin leather is used. Should a thick leather be used it must be thoroughly wetted on both sides—a thin leather is preferable and needs only damping on the back; it should be taken in the left hand, with three fingers supporting it underneath, and the thumb and first finger on the top. A suitable modeller or a tool with a steel ball is then used (the writer prefers the former) to work up the design from the back, gently working it backwards and forwards until the desired relief is obtained—this entirely depends upon the taste of the individual, but it should not be forgotten that high relief tends to give a vulgar effect to embossed work. The above is the usual method adopted, but there are several others. The leather may be placed face *upwards* on a sheet of wax, worked out quite flat on a card or wooden tray. The wax should be prepared with spirit, or a thin piece of grease-proof paper should be placed between the wax and leather to avoid a greasy stain. Yet another method is to trace the design on the under side of the leather, and, after damping, to place it on the wax, face *downwards*, and work the *design* with the modeller where the embossed effect is required, the wax beneath giving way under the pressure. Or, again, the leather may be similarly placed upon a pad made of chamois leather, filled with fine sand to a thickness of about a half or three-quarters of an inch; the pad should feel tight when filled, otherwise the sand will give way too much under pressure. The working in this method is the same as on the wax. After the design has been embossed, the modelling and finishing on the front surface must be done. The leather should be turned face upwards and well damped, the outlines emphasised either by opening, or, if not cut, by the use of a modelling tool, going over the outlines to correct or clearly define with the edge of the tool; all hard lines should be softened, stems and leaves sharpened up and shaded and varied as much as the worker's knowledge of modelling dictates, and the work examined critically and carefully, going over every portion thoughtfully (still keeping the leather damp). The modelling tool should be used to work down the background smoothly all round the design, to give a greater effect of relief. It is not necessary to pad when the embossing is slight. For those who emboss with portions in very high relief.

FIG. 13.—FOR THE STUDY OF DIFFERENT PLANES.

FIG. 14.—BALL TOOL

Modelled Work.—Although modelling is here made a separate article, yet it enters into all methods of relief leather decoration, and is not only the most interesting part of the work, but gives the widest scope for originality, artistic treatment and personal feeling, and can be brought to the level of the very best wax modelling. It is rather difficult to explain in writing, and needs *personal* instruction more than most methods.

The tools required are few and simple—the marble slab, tracer and several modellers of various widths and different curves. These latter are better when made of brass, or nickelled. Steel is apt to cause black stains on the leather if the latter is a little too damp.

Figs. 15, 16, and 17 are illustrations of useful modellers.

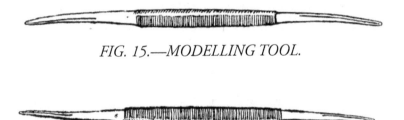

FIG. 15.—MODELLING TOOL.

FIG. 16.—MODELLING TOOL.

FIG. 17.—DRESDEN TOOL.

The design is transferred on to the skin in the way described for incised work. Modelled work may be produced with an incised line, which helps to give a greater effect of relief—or by a traced one, strengthened with an opener or the edge of a modelling tool. For this work, thick calf or even cowhide may be used, so as to obtain as much relief as possible. Indeed, its beauty lies in the amount of relief obtained, combined with the softness, variety, and delicacy of modelling, such as is found in wax or clay low relief. To facilitate the work of this relief modelling, the surface should be kept constantly moist and thereby more plastic. After strengthening the outlines with the modelling tool or opener, proceed to bring out and accentuate the design by lowering the surrounding background. Always keep the leather damp, press the flat side of the tool firmly down as it is passed over the leather (using the incision or line as a guide), producing the relief effect by judicious pressings in the same way as wax or clay. Thus, say the design includes a large curved leaf, depress the inner portion *a* (Fig. 18) and elevate the outer margin *b*, round off the portion *c* where the leaf curves, and depress the inner portion *d*, leaving *e* as high as possible. Or, if a scroll is to be modelled, depress the portion turning under at *a* and *b* (Fig. 19), allowing *c* to stand as high as possible; *e* would be lower than *c*, but not so low as *b*, and so on, *d* being lightly lower than *c*. Keep before the mind's eye a picture of what the finished design *should be*, and use every action of the modelling tool to bring it up to this. Of course, to do this really well, a certain amount of artistic ability is essential. A student who has studied modelling will naturally be the most successful, but even if this is absent, very excellent results can be obtained where a good design is selected for reproduction. If the modelling is successful, the design should, when finished, have the appearance of a modelled wax plaque. The great charm of modelled leather lies in the clearness and softness of its forms and outlines, and care must be taken to avoid irregularities either in incising or modelling—especially with stems, and lines in borders, as these disagreeably arrest the eye by failing to merge into the ground.

FIG. 18.—A CURVED LEAF.

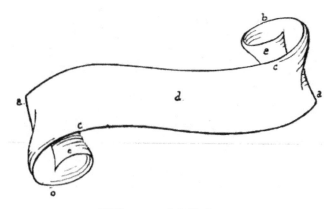

FIG. 19.—A SCROLL.

The modelling may also be done by placing the skin upon a bed of wax and working down the background, leaving the design in relief, and then touching up the latter according to the taste and ability of the worker. This method is easy, and one whereby even an inexperienced worker may, with care, do some effective work.

Carved Work.—We have already remarked that this method of decorating leather is extremely difficult and should not be attempted by the amateur. If, however, any of our readers desire to attempt it, we may mention one or two points for their guidance.

Very thick and firm leather should be used (preferably cowhide), and the outline of the design cut much deeper than for ordinary incised work. The same knife may be used for this purpose, but another is necessary with the blade sharpened all round the point; this is for undercutting where high relief is required, as, for instance, for a curled leaf, a helmet front, or in any case where it is desired that one part should stand boldly forward. After these undercuts have been carefully modelled up, they must be padded in the manner to be described under this heading later on.

PLATE IV

ALTAR SERVICE, MODELLED.

The details of the design are then incised and modelled in the ordinary way, the cuts not being so deep as the outlines, the incisions are clearly opened and the background pressed well down from the design and punched—thus producing the effect of relief in wood-carving.

Hammered or Punched Work.—Having already dealt with the different modes of producing decoration in relief, we will now explain how the richness and finish of the design may be materially increased. There are several ways of doing this, but by far the more important is the ornamentation of backgrounds by the use of steel punches. Not only does this give greater beauty to the work, but it also serves very greatly to accentuate the relief as well as making the leather more durable. Punches are made in many different forms, and the patterns which may be produced with their aid, either singly or in combination, are practically unlimited. Subjoined are illustrations of a few of the most useful.

In using a punch great care must be taken to keep it perfectly upright, as otherwise the impression left on the leather will be incomplete and unsatisfactory. A small hammer is used with the punch, and, with this, a gentle but sharp tap is given *flat on the head of the punch.* If the stroke is not made true—*i.e.* if on the edge of the punch or the side of the hammer instead of the centre—a slovenly impression results, a portion of the pattern being almost invisible, and the remainder forced too deeply into the leather.

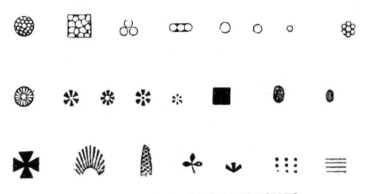

FIG. 20.—DESIGNS FOR PUNCHES.

The edge of the punch must be placed against the outline of the raised design, and on no account should the outline itself be infringed upon.

The most useful punches are those producing a small check or powdered design in mat form. In using these, it is not at all necessary that the impressions should be made in any regular order; they may slightly overlap, so that the whole background is well covered, but not so even as to look machine-like, and the punching may be closely packed behind and around the work, and only a powdering further round.

Punches, such as the dots, wavy lines, pearls, stars, etc., shown in Fig. 20, are used in Mexican decoration for accentuating parts of the design.

A pretty effect may be produced by varnishing on the punched depressions, and then painting them with bronze or gouache.

Mosaic Work.—Several styles of leather decoration, all needing great care and nicety, may be included under this heading; and no one who lacks patience would be wise to attempt any of them. We shall only explain here a couple of the most simple methods.

Mosaic work consists of the inlay and the background: for the inlay, a thin calf or split sheep is used, preferably the former; for the background, a grained leather is the best, as it shows up the inlay more advantageously.

Thoroughly good paste is essential, and can be obtained at the saddler's; or that recommended at the end of the Chapter on "Making Up" may be used. Seccotine or gum must never be employed.

Having procured some leather for the background, paste it on to a piece of firm, smooth millboard, fairly thick. If the size is large, it will probably cause the board to curl, in which case a sheet of paper should be pasted on the reverse side in order to draw the board the other way. Put the prepared board somewhere to press; if no proper press is available, lay it on an even flat table, with a sheet of zinc, or smooth, heavy board over it, and weights so arranged as to distribute the pressure evenly over the whole surface; leave it under pressure until quite dry.

Split sheep-skin is so extremely thin that, if used for inlaying, it must be strengthened in some way to allow the cutting to be successfully managed; the best way is slightly and evenly to paste strong paper (not too thick) on to the surface of the leather—using paste diluted with half the quantity of water, and beaten to a cream, and quite free from lumps. This must be carefully done, and so that adhesion is only slight, in order that the paper may be damped and removed when the work is finished. Smooth out any wrinkles with the folder, and then place under pressure to dry.

PLATE V

BOOK-COVER, MODELLED WITH PUNCHED BACK-GROUND.

The design is traced on to the paper with a hard, sharp-pointed pencil and carbon paper. There are several knives suitable for cutting out; those used by stencil-cutters are suitable, but the student will find that the small, pen-shaped knives, which may be obtained from a photographic outfitter's in boxes of a dozen, are most useful; they can be firmly fixed in a penholder, which is more comfortable to use than the metal holder supplied.

Place the work on a stiff piece of fine cardboard (not millboard, which might spoil the knife), hold the knife firmly in a fairly upright position, just as a pen should be held, but slightly inclined to the right. The cutting is done—not by moving the knife, which is to be kept stationary—but *by moving the leather with the left hand*, keeping two fingers on the surface and the thumb and third and fourth fingers underneath, and gently and carefully drawing it under the knife so as to ensure a perfectly clean cut. Especial care should be used in cutting corners and curves, and on no account should an attempt be made to separate by pulling, as the edge would then stretch and look untidy. When the work is too large to manage in this way, it should be pinned to the cardboard, and both moved as described, in which case a polished table, large piece of glass, or marble slab will be required.

Cut the bolder portions first, working from the centre, and leaving stems and smaller details until the last. Next, take the cut-out design and place it on to the background in the right position, and press it well, so that the design is marked with a clear outline; it will be found that the paper support is a great advantage at this point. Now make a smooth paste of starch of the consistency of thick cream (mix with cold water, and add boiling water until it turns clear); brush over the exposed side of the cut-out design with this, taking care that not the slightest spot is missed: the work will be easier if drawing pins are used, so that the *heads* hold it firmly and prevent curling. Damp the groundwork with water where the design is to be placed, and then carefully lay the cut-out portion into position and press with the hand, except where the fine stems or points need a modelling tool; then with a roller go over the whole, placing a piece of thin paper between the work and the roller as a protection. Place it under slight pressure for a few minutes, and allow time to dry. The paper on the surface of the design may now be damped sufficiently to allow it to be removed. But care must be taken to prevent pulling up the inlay; if this should occur, it must be at once replaced with fresh paste, and worked back to its proper size with the modelling tool. After the paper has all been removed, the whole must be washed over (using as little moisture as possible), and placed under boards to dry.

The next step is, by outlining the work, to lose or disguise the line where the design meets the background. A tool, called an outliner, is used, with the rounded side towards the design and just within it, half on the inlay and half on the background. The leather is worked down with the tool—cold at first, and afterwards slightly heated; when this is properly done, the edge of the inlay is lost in the groove thus formed. Where straight lines are required, it is better to use the square end of the tool.

The second method is more suitable for designs of a bolder

type. In this work the design is traced on to the background and cut out in the manner before described; it is then placed on to a piece of leather decided upon for the inlay, using it as a pattern to cut out the design which will fill in the space cut in the background. If a velvet Persian, velvet calf, or any thin or soft leather is used, the thin paper support will be needed, but this time on the back, where it may remain to strengthen it.

The background leather is placed face downwards on to cardboard, or a smooth drawing-board, the cut-out design (also face downwards) is placed into position, and a thin paper pared very thin at the edges, or fine muslin frayed at the edges, pasted on to the back to ensure the design keeping in place, until the outline on the surface has been worked in with the outliner to disguise and strengthen the join.

The piece of leather cut out of the background and used as a pattern for cutting the inlay may be used as an inlay for another background.

Students who prefer to paint in the gold instead of using the leaf may mix pure gold powder with gum and water to a creamy consistency and paint on as one would any body colour, and when dry, quickly and thinly varnish with a mixture of one part Jap gold size and three parts turpentine.

CHAPTER IV

COLOURING AND STAINING

AFTER a design has been worked out on the leather, the work may of course be "made up" as it is; but the addition of colour, in some form, so greatly improves the appearance, that most students will desire to adopt it. The beginner will be wise at first to restrict himself to simple flat washes, in two or three subdued tones; later on, he may, if he has any experience in ordinary colour work, produce very charming effects by a more elaborate form of decoration.

It is true that staining or laying on of simple washes is rather nervous work, as uniformity of colour is in most cases absolutely essential—we say in most cases, because this remark does not apply when a mottled appearance is required; but attention to the following instructions, and a little patience, will soon enable the worker to overcome all difficulties.

First of all the entire surface of the leather must be well and uniformly damped with water, and *an amply sufficient* supply of the stain prepared by diluting the colouring fluid with water or methylated spirit,* according as water or spirit stains are used. It should be borne in mind that the desired tone is to be produced, not by a single application of the stain, but by several repetitions, so that the wash should be quite pale and not of the full tone required. All being ready, a large soft brush, preferably cheap dark sable, is well filled with the liquid, and rapidly and evenly passed over the part to be coloured, *with a circular motion*, and then any excess lightly removed with a piece of soft linen or old washing silk, in order to prevent hard lines from forming. In colouring large surfaces, a soft sponge or small pad of cotton-wool, wrapped in soft linen, may advantageously be substituted for the brush. If the final colouring is darker than is desired, the leather should be dipped in water and scrubbed with a soft brush and soft soap, but this is by no means to be recommended; after a little practice, the evil is not likely to occur. Having stained the background, the design itself is taken in hand. For this, the colours are to be diluted as before, and carefully applied with a smaller brush— not too full, as it is important to avoid any colour going on to the background; as each brushful is put on, quickly and softly wipe with the rag, to remove any excess of fluid. Although the background has been here mentioned as being coloured quite separately from the design, it does not follow that it will be done in this order, as it may be necessary to go from one to the other, over and over again, until a perfect result is obtained. Finally, when the whole of the staining is done, a very pale wash of the background tint may with advantage be brushed over *the entire surface* of the work: this brings the whole together, and greatly adds to the effect.

There are various methods of producing special effects, such as sprinkling, marbling, shading, etc. Sprinkling is done with a long, narrow brush and metal sprinkler; the brush is filled with stain, and rubbed backwards and forwards over the sprinkler, an inch or two above the leather surface, scattering on it a fine shower of colour. For marbling a sponge with large holes is filled with dye, and lightly dabbed over the leather, so that parts are left ur touched. Shading is easily produced by working the colour on with a circular motion and different shades of stain.

* The French now sell a variety of tints *in powder*, to be mixed as required: these are convenient where much colouring has to be done, but for beginners, small bottles of ready-prepared fluids are sufficient.

CHAPTER V

GILDING

WE do not propose to deal here with gold tooling as practised by the bookbinder—namely with hot tools—but to suggest a means of lighting up an otherwise dull scheme of colour, or to enrich an uncoloured piece of work. It is not often that this kind of tooling is needed, but there are times when a touch of gold will make an otherwise uninteresting article into something really beautiful.

Gold leaf may be applied to parts of a design, such as the centres of flowers, or a punched background to a design, enclosed in panel form, may have gold leaf applied and rubbed off when nearly dry, leaving the gold in the depressions made by the punch.

In using this type of decoration, the student must use great restraint, being careful to avoid a spotty effect or the overpowering of the work by too liberal an application.

Procure from an artists' colourman a packet of concentrated size, a bottle of Japanese gold size, and a book of gold leaf transferred on to waxed leaves, and have ready some soft, white cotton-wool. The cushion and brush usually employed may quite well be dispensed with.

For leather which has not been coloured, a solution of the concentrated size must be prepared by mixing a good teaspoonful of size with boiling water until fairly thin, but sufficiently strong to feel sticky on the finger. When cool, paint this on to the design or background, where the gold is to be applied, and, if the leather takes up the size too rapidly, give it a second coat, but it must not look thick or even show a film. Several layers of starch paste are sometimes as effective.

Let the size dry, after which paint on a coat of Japanese gold size, and, as soon as this is nearly dry, but still sticky, take the gold leaf and cut it into suitable sizes for handling easily (the whole leaf may be used if carefully managed). Next lift it with a knife made for this work, or, failing this, with the tip of the finger or the tip of a penknife, and with great care lay it on to the place to be decorated and very gently press with a soft pad of cotton-wool.

It would be wise here to point out that only a portion of the work at a time should have the Japanese gold size painted on; if warm, dry weather, very little; if cool or damp weather, a larger amount. This is necessary to ensure that the size does not become too dry to allow the gold to adhere.

When using gold leaf on leather, it is sometimes necessary to go over the surface a second time with the leaf, and it will be found, if done at once, that breathing gently on the spot will soften the size sufficiently to take the second layer. This, of course, does not apply if the size is left to dry first.

When a background is to be rubbed off the surface of the punching, it must be allowed almost to dry, or the gold will become dulled. On the other hand, should it be found to be too dry, a slight touch of turpentine on a soft fine piece of rag or cotton-wool will help to remove the superfluous gold, to break up the surface and leave only the gold which has been pressed into the tool marks.

When gilding work which has already been coloured and has probably had several coats of stain and become polished, it will generally be found unnecessary to use the first size as mentioned above, because the pores of the leather have already become sealed. In this case the Japanese gold is painted on to a larger portion of the leather, as the size will take longer to dry on the slightly polished surface.

CHAPTER VI

PADDING FOR EMBOSSED WORK

ANY design which has parts in bold relief worked up from the back needs some filling or support at the back, to preserve these in shape. The material used for this filling varies. Some prefer a special wax, which is sold in thick sticks; it should be slightly warmed, and then small pieces pulled off, and smeared, as it were, in layers, in the hollows, until they are filled up—the work being laid for the purpose on a flat surface. Other fillings are made of absorbent cotton-wool soaked in flour-and-water paste, or cuttings of kid-skins (or old gloves), shredded very fine and mixed with talc or dextrine.

A good filling is made as follows: Take some of the odd remnants of leather (cow or calf-skin) that you may have by you, and, with a "paring knife" (*see* Chapter on "Making Up") pare or scrape off *soft*, flaky pieces from the back, avoiding all lumps or thick slices. When you have pared what you fancy will be enough, it will be quite safe to do as much again, as the cuttings, when made up, shrink to a very small compass. Mix these parings with the flour-and-water paste, thinned down with water, or mix to a creamy consistency with dextrine or talc, and the filling is ready for use.

Another padding may be made by mixing sawdust and rye-meal with thin flour paste, but this is not to be recommended.

Great care is necessary to avoid using an excess of the padding, whatever it may be, as otherwise unsightly wrinkling may show all round the design when it is made up. The mixture should, therefore, be kept moist, and any excess smoothed off evenly with a wet knife.

For flowers, stems, or other long straight lines, a good padding is made by dipping a piece of twine or cord of suitable thickness into a bowl of ordinary paste, and laying in the proper position. For undercut portions on the surface (mentioned in "Carved Work"), the leather scraped as explained, and mixed with creamy paste water, is the best. Of course it must be cleaned off the surface all round with a damp soft sponge; it is impossible to pad on the surface without slightly soiling surrounding parts.

CHAPTER VII

MAKING UP

WE wish we could assure the reader that it is quite easy to get decorated leather made up into the articles for which it is intended. Except for small articles such as pocket-books, purses, blotting-cases, etc., it is unfortunately not so, and these the worker may easily make up for him or herself, if attention is given to the following simple instructions. For larger things, the writer will at all times be glad to give advice as to the best means to adopt, knowing all too well how exceedingly irritating it is to have one's handiwork—often perhaps the result of weeks of loving care—absolutely ruined by a stupid or careless mechanic devoid of a spark of artistic feeling. Unless one is prepared to expend a considerable sum in presses, tools, etc., one has to incur this risk; but some firms give special attention to this class of work, and one or two may be recommended with confidence.

PLATE VI

BLOTTING-CASE, CUT AND MODELLED,

Tools.—For making up simple things, the tools required are: a paring-knife, a cutter (which may be used also as a parer), set square, an awl, edge-parer, marking tool, bone folder, pair of scissors, cutting-board, some saddler's pointless needles, and some saddler's or tailor's silk.

A skin or two of lining leather will be required. Calf is much the best, but is rather expensive; Persian calf is less so, and nearly as good. The cheapest and most generally used is sheep, and we recommend the student to commence with this.

Let us assume that a blotting-case has been worked, and has to be made up. The following brief hints will enable this to be done, and will apply equally to a card-case or wallet.

Lay the worked leather face upwards on the cutting-board, and, with the set square and a flat rule, proceed first to prove all lines and corners. If these are true, then a slight line should be marked all round, to indicate where a narrow strip of leather shall be removed, in order to make a clean true edge. In doing this, the knife should be kept upright, to ensure that the cut is clean and straight.

Edges.—A word of explanation about these. They may be either pared thin and turned over, or kept square—or raw— and sewn with thread or silk; the latter method wears better, and we will describe this first.

Turn the leather face downwards on the marble, and, with an edge-parer, remove the edges and any roughness, so that all may look quite smooth and not clumsy when finished. At the same time, pare away some of the thickness of the leather where the fold will come to form the back. Next prepare a piece of lining leather of the same size as the work, and, having this at hand, well paste over the back of the worked leather with bookbinder's paste, taking care to avoid any lumps or ridges (*see* end of Chapter as to this paste). Carefully and evenly place the lining leather on to this, and lightly smooth down to prevent wrinkles forming; lay a sheet of clean paper over, and, with the folder, go gently over the whole surface to ensure uniform adhesion, keeping the paper in place with the left hand: do not press too heavily, lest the lining leather should stretch. Having done this, place the work under pressure on an even surface—say on a drawing-board, with another similar board and some books on it and a sheet of paper over the face of the work to protect it. Just enough pressure should be put on as will ensure perfect adhesion, but not risk spoiling the design; leave until quite dry, and in the meantime proceed to prepare the pocket. To do this, cut a piece of Persian calf leather a trifle larger than the size required, and pare away about half an inch of the underside of one of the long edges. The paring-knife should be very sharp, and held in the hand with the blade as flat as possible: the paring is done by *pushing* strokes, cutting away a shaving at a time, and *gradually* thinning down the leather towards the edge, so that, when doubled, the pared part shall be little more than the natural thickness of the skin. Then, with a folder, turn the leather sharply over against the edge of a rule and well mark the fold; thoroughly paste the underside, and rub the fold down under a piece of paper until adhesion is complete. The three other edges may now be pasted, and, the work having been removed from the press, the pocket may be placed in position on the lined blotter, and pressed till dry, when it is ready for stitching.

Stitching.—This may be done by hand or with a sewing-machine, but many prefer handwork. Take a marking tool (Fig. 21), and carefully make a series of distance marks, about a sixteenth of an inch from the edge, to indicate where the stitches are to come Without this, it is impossible to obtain really neat regular stitching. Then pierce through the marks with a saddler's awl, taking care always to keep the tool in the same position, so that the holes may look uniform. A hard pad or cushion of felt, about an inch thick, or a piece of soft cork, is helpful for this purpose.

With some hot-water starch, thinned well down with water, damp the edges, and afterwards polish with a firm pad of soft flannel or linen. It will improve the appearance if a sharp line be made on each side of the stitching, and quite close to it, with the edge of a modeller or a tool known as a screw-crease.

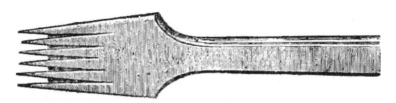

FIG. 21.—MARKING TOOL.

The actual stitching may be accomplished either with two needles or a single one. Beginners had better be content at first with the latter. Use good, well-twisted silk—not thick, like buttonhole twist, or thin, like ordinary machine silk; saddler's or tailor's silk is best if obtainable. It is not wise to take a long thread, thinking to avoid a join; in most cases a join is unavoidable, and in any case the silk would become roughened and possibly unravel before reaching the end. Pass the needle in and out of the holes in such a way that a space is left between each stitch made; work all round a second time in the same manner, filling in the blank spaces—the stitches will then look alike on both sides, and have a finished appearance.

Another method—with two needles—is the more correct way of working, but this needs some special arrangement for holding the work (as saddlers do), so that both hands may be free. A needle is held in each hand, and both are passed in opposite directions (*i.e.* point to point) through the same holes; both hands are thus engaged, and both threads are to be pulled through simultaneously (but on opposite sides) and evenly; the stitches throughout are thus made quite uniform.

The final step is to finish off the ends of the silk neatly; to do this, sew over several of the first stitches, and then, drawing the ends out, between the leather and lining, fray them, paste, and push back between the two leathers, and press together again. Some prefer simply to tie the ends of silk together when stitching is finished, and not to sew back as recommended, but the above is neater and more workmanlike.

Leather Stitching.—This is worked with very narrow thongs cut from Persian calf (or very thin ordinary calf), threaded through holes made with a round cutter or punch, which can be purchased, together with a holder into which it is fixed, at any good tool-maker's. The holes should be punched about a quarter of an inch from the edge, and about the same distance apart, the leather thong being threaded or laced through, to form an oversewing at the edge. With a little practice, the student should be able to cut the thongs quite fine enough for ordinary work—for small articles very fine ones can be purchased, but usually only by sending abroad for them. A fork-like tool is sometimes used for making the holes; but it is not to be recommended, as it is very difficult to manage. All sizes can be obtained in the round punches. When doing *leather stitching*—the edges should be polished before punching the holes.

Turned-over Edges.—The procedure for turned-over edges is as follows. About half an inch of leather is allowed all round the work, beyond the size required when finished; this and a little more must be carefully pared away in the manner already described, taking a graduated shaving very evenly off each edge. When the actual edges are pared to the thinness of paper, any ruggedness must be trimmed off neatly with knife and rule.

Lining.—The lining is then put on—having first had about a quarter of an inch of each edge pared very thin—and finally the pocket is added; the three sides which are not turned in having also been pared, they are slightly pasted at the edge and placed into position—namely, the actual size required, and a little less than the worked leather. The pared edges of the worked leather itself are then pasted and turned down on to the lining, the corners being carefully mitred, and all well rubbed down with the folder, using paper between for protection. Press and leave to dry; then, with a creaser or beveller, make a clear sharp line over the junction of the turned piece with lining, thus disguising as well as better securing the join.

One word about the lining. If this should stretch, or prove to have been cut larger than required, it must be carefully trimmed off before the final finishing off is attempted.

Blotting cases are made with either one or two pockets, and sometimes a second pocket (smaller) is stitched on the face of the pocket to take envelopes, etc., before it is attached to the case. A piece of broad elastic or strip of leather, should be inserted down the back to hold the blotting-paper. This can be pasted at each end, and carefully caught in at the same time as the stitching is done.

It would be too lengthy here to explain how to make up boxes, caskets, etc., but those who wish to try should buy the necessary wooden box ready made, or, if millboard is preferred, obtain pieces cut to size required from a bookbinder; glue the edges together after paring (or mitreing) them (sometimes it is necessary to bind the joins with thin paper or very thin linen); then take the leather and work as with "turned-over edges" explained already, and, when all is turned in, make the lining neatly finish off at the edges. Where each side is a separate piece, a great deal of paring will be needed at the corners, one being wrapped round (which must be as thin as the thinnest paper) and the other cut off and worked down exactly *at* the corner.

Paste.—Before closing this chapter, it will be well to give a recipe for making paste. Take two ounces of good flour and rather less than a quarter of a teaspoonful of alum, mix with a little water; add a pint of cold water, place in an enamelled saucepan, bring slowly to boiling-point, stirring all the time, and let it continue to boil for five minutes. When cold it is ready for use, and will keep well for some time. If it becomes too thick, it may be let down with a little water.

CPSIA information can be obtained
at www.ICGtesting.com
Printed in the USA
LVHW111051020919
629634LV00003B/973/P